Autotheory

~~a theory of memory & time~~

poems, i guess

ishaan saxena

INDIA · SINGAPORE · MALAYSIA

ISBN 979-8-89133-890-6

Note to the Reader

Why do we write? We write to preserve our memories and we write to forget our grief. To fill the space on the empty page. To pass the time on our longer nights. We write to ask questions, and we write to search for answers. Writing has not one, but several functions in our individual and our collective lives, and it is not an act that can be reduced to a singular purpose or essence—much like our being itself.

Why I write, likewise, is not something I could describe in a word, or even in the length of a page. However, I hope that a glimpse of this can be found somewhere in this book. In the five self-contained sections that follow, I present a collection of my writings from the early years of my adult life. I call this collection Autotheory.

What do I mean by Autotheory? This is by no means a novel term. Apart from the obvious connotation as a blend of auto and theory, meaning a theory of the self, the word has been present in literary spheres since the late 2000s where it has come to gather a slightly different connotation. This interprets the word as a framework that critiques and challenges dominant perspectives through the use of subjective and autobiographical material. It is a critical artistic practice.

Words carry weight. Words build our worlds, and they show us the way through it. Words help us find ourselves and our homes in this chaos that we are all condemned to navigate. In that spirit, Autotheory is an attempt to use words from my pen to reimagine the world we live in, to rediscover the world we share with each other.

Even so, these words are merely a vessel. They can shape the meaning that comes, but all meaning must be poured. This much I shall leave to you, dear reader. To pour meaning into these words, or even into our lives, is a complex task, but it is one that must begin in a search. That is to say, *my principal aim has been to start a process of questioning*—of searching for connections and paths that guide us through all time and space. "Philosophy must be done as poetry. To uncover the world, one must rediscover the ways of seeing it."

— Ishaan

Delhi, 2023

for all my friends and all my lovers, named and unnamed,

for all the tender memories playing closely in sync with my heartbeat,

for all the lovely kisses spaced unevenly on my flesh,

and for you, who lent them to me

for as long as we lay here

सूची | Contents | فہرست

اک رات وہ گیا تھا جہاں بات روک کے
اب تک رکا ہوا ہوں وہیں رات روک کے

فرحت احساس

इक रात वो गया था जहाँ बात रोक के
अब तक रुका हुआ हूँ वहीं रात रोक के

फ़रहत एहसास

Autotheory

Rituals

a prayer in blue

Rituals

1.   The world is everything that is the case. (Wittgenstein).

2.   I do not take Wittgenstein too seriously. I do not know many who choose to do so either.

3.   One should not be too quick to draw any conclusions from this fact. Most of my friends find themselves on the fringes of the vast fields of life—most of my friends wear ripped clothing. That's how they bought it. It will be handy tonight. Most of my friends could not give a fuck.

     Safia pours four shots for the two of us. She had a long day at work. Four more? Safia paints my eyelids with the most luscious red and we dress up in its other extravagant shades. We meet Hannah and Sid at the L train. We go to raves on Tuesday nights. Wednesday mornings? There is little difference for us. We work, we play. We have been condemned to this life. Our life. Most of my friends could not give a fuck about what Wittgenstein had to say when our problems are so clearly much more important than whatever some random old white dude in the 20th century was talking about.

4.   That is to say there is no one truth. My friends form an almost insignificant sample of the entirety of things. A small sample is seldom sufficient to see the image form. All flowers bloom, some less blue than others, some more. That is to say there is no one blue.

5.   Blue is good. I am not certain what *good* means yet, but I have been blue, so blue must be good.

6.   The truth is, that I have always wanted to be good. Whose eyes measure my goodness, though, has often varied. And with this I too change in somewhat mysterious ways. It is always the glimmer in these eyes that makes me want to be good.

     It is the frequent fleeting caresses of your hand that show me *it must be* a virtue to make popcorn before the film. It is that smell of orange peel and basil on the base of your palm, and in the depths of my memory, who still helps me pick out pleasant candles at Target. It is only your moan that reminds me how fucking good fucking can be.

Why I want to be good is perhaps a truth better unpacked in a therapy session than in a book.

7. Whereof one cannot speak, thereof one must remain silent.

8. I say I do not take Wittgenstein too seriously, yet this last proposition is etched into my skin with blank ink. Natalie did the whole piece in just under half an hour in her incense-fumed Brooklyn studio. It was long enough for her to realize that all my tattoos shortly followed heartbreak or a similar ailment. I didn't even have to utter it, that much she had gathered from my unusual silence.

9. The unuttered will be—*unutterably*—contained in what has been uttered. *And in what hasn't.*

10. The eyes are the surface that reveal the incredible depths of the soul. The soul is the hope that keeps me opening my eyes for yet another day. The silence of the eye of the silent soul speaking the unspeakable.

    When the eye is watching, it is most likely a matter of great concern to the soul.

11. Some rules in our emergency handbook are unwritten. One simply could not write all the rules.

12. People who think they can write down all the rules are stupid. I know they are stupid. They just had to be. *But still, let me try my hand at this.* Berkeley was wrong about the tree in the forest. Berkeley being wrong was wrong itself, since Berkeley never actually said "If a tree falls in a forest...". Of course, it was wrong. It is all wrong.

13. In many ways writing a book is like a therapy session.

14. Or maybe it's not. I wouldn't know; it just sounded like a not-wrong thing to say. Really–I just wanted to say that to sound profound, as if I could offer an interesting insight into something in the world. As if I could be the light at the end of the tunnel. Many men have pretended to know the world. They have written countless books to demonstrate their knowledge, perhaps themselves trying to evade expensive therapy. I can't share these pretensions. There is a tunnel. But I don't have a light. I am the moth roaming within it, hungry, scared. I get lost with every new step–do you know which way is the way out of here?

15. Perhaps I just wrote that to remind myself that I don't really need to go to therapy (*lie*).

16. Perhaps I just wrote that to remind myself that if I wrote a book I wouldn't really need to go to therapy (*lie*).

17. Perhaps I just wrote that to remind myself that if someday you read these letters I am writing, you will start to love me again, and then I really wouldn't really need to go to therapy (*indeterminate*).

18. A *random walk* is a mathematical game. A game of chances. Starting at a point, the random walk randomly walks a unit step in a unit direction at a unit time interval. If the random walk ever returns home, it is said to be convergent.

19. The laws of mathematics curiously apply differently in different dimensions. *Different truths?* A random walk in one or two dimensions may converge, but a random walk in three or more almost never will. *The same truth, repeated with differences?*

20. A drunk mouse may return home, but a drunk moth will forever keep stumbling:

    will wake, read, write long letters
    and wander the alleys up and down
    restlessly, like a leaf in the wind. (Rilke).

21. I was certain I had to change how I am to be good. But whose eyes should I listen to? My father's saw me only how he wished, my mother's avoided my gaze. Is there a God watching us? Do your eyes still linger even after all these years? And what if those eyes had hurt you? If your eyes don't recall opening up to mine, and if your gaze only remembers my face as it turns away, is there any good reason to trust them? If there are no eyes looking, is there even a *good* anyway? If a tsunami hits the shore and there's no one there to see it, it does make a sound, but that tsunami is not what we would call a catastrophic disaster.

22. All concepts depend on the existence of others. Some concepts depend on the existence of you and me. *Disaster. Hurt. Good. Fuck. Love.*

23. I am tempted to think that when Maggie Nelson wrote *Bluets* she was carefully mistranslating Wittgenstein's *Tractatus* through a blue-tinted

lens. Rewriting it in blue ink. *This seems unimaginable, but the fact is that it happens all the time.* I take these blues seriously. I take all sorts of love seriously and her love for the blues was a serious one.

24. I like to read Wittgenstein like poetry. I am not the only poet who takes an interest in Wittgenstein. Elisa Gabbert asks the only reasonable question—*was Wittgenstein sexy?* After some deliberation, she concludes that the answer is either "yes" or "unanswerable".

    Wittgenstein too, might point out that, just like a Tuesday night that fades into a Wednesday morning, good poetry and good philosophy have little difference. I think this is quite sexy.

25. If I am to, for a second, take Wittgenstein seriously, and assume that the universe is everything that there is (this seems a fair assumption), then I am tempted to think God too lives somewhere in this universe. If God is not within you and me, then she must be in the spaces in between. In the emptiness. Is her body the dark matter you are looking for? I suppose it is indeed a bit hard to find God. But I imagine God could not be a part of the universe. For God is all-encompassing. God created the world. The world is everything that is the case... Then it must be the case that the God is the whole world. The whole world is the whole God. (An equivalence!).

26. God is the first mother. She whose body is so majestic, if she had to be buried her body could only be buried within itself.

    Her body, the site of all our hours. Her tomb, the site of all ours.

27. Spinoza, in his writings, always wrote God/Nature instead of the universe. He believed it is the only *substance* (a thing that can exist independently of all things). I think it is reasonable to think that God and the universe are the same thing. Alas, I seem to forget the last time I bent my knee or laid my face against Mihrab on my woolen prayer mat. The wool which now resembles a pale iodide salt deposited on a steel mesh. It lays packed away in my mother's basement. My mother who now resembles a pale iodide salt deposited on an iron nail. My mother, who taught me the last prayer I remembered. That last prayer, forgotten.

    If I ever pray to a God again, though, I think I will keep Spinoza's God in my mind.

28. Kaveh Akbar wrote "Any text that is not a holy text is an apostasy. [...] Then it is a holy text." I have read these propositions over and over and I find nothing holy within them.

29. It is with these propositions, my rituals, that I wish to relearn divinity. This is my prayer.

30. *God's word is a melody, and a melody requires repetition.*
God's word is a melody, I sang once and then I forgot. (Kaveh Akbar).

31. Rituals require repetition.

32. Wittgenstein would repeatedly claim that any totality would always have an inexpressible character. Clearly, Wittgenstein had been in love. Any set of symbols, words, languages, would fail to adequately capture this ever-evolving shape-shifting totality. (admittedly, I am actually still uncertain if this totality can even be or even be—evolving or shifting or ever or shape).

33. All that can be said, can be said clearly, our torchbearer claims. This much the sciences could do. To him, the project of philosophy was thus clear.

    Everything that cannot be said must be passed down in silence.
    Everything that cannot be said can be shown.

34. Philosophy must be done as poetry.

    To uncover the world, one must rediscover the ways of seeing it.

35. What Wittgenstein had just discovered was already known to Ra'bia al'Adawiyya in the younger years of the sun. Perhaps this is a part of the reason I do not take Wittgenstein seriously. (whiteness)

36. Kaveh Akbar wrote "Any text that is not a holy text is an apostasy. [...] Then it is a holy text."

37. If God is indeed this totality that is the universe, then Ra'bia had long started Wittgenstein's philosophical project. With every breath, Ra'bia spoke to and spoke of only her beloved. With every word, she serenaded her beloved with utter devotion. Aware completely of the inexpressibility of this love, this mysterious celestial process, her words of devotion still contained—*inexpressibly*—this inexpressible. Her words a divine daguerreotype.

38. "Ironic, but one of the most intimate acts of our body is death." She
wrote. I wonder if she knew that the French called orgasms *la petit mort*
or "a little death". All my orgasms colored blue by the light that shines
through your curtains as my eyes can barely stay open anymore. Is it in
death that one is safe with their beloved?

39. Her words that now resemble a pale iodide salt deposited on a cosmic
grave.

40. *Any text that is not a holy text is an apostasy…* I have read these propositions
over and over and I find nothing holy within them.

41. I try hard to keep my eyes open.

I hope I can catch your eyes glimmering in that blue light.
Somewhere in time they look back at mine.
Somewhere in this time, I was seen, loved, found.
I replay this time and call it a memory.
I keep it close to my chest.
I replay this memory and call it a hope.
With every heartbeat–almost in sync with the rhythm of a clock–
I replay this hope and call it my soul.

42. When Ra'bia wrote *my beloved*, she thought of God. When I write it,
my tongue prepares itself to speak your name. I have been careful to
omit it, but that does not mean my love is any less divine.

Autotheory

زندگی تو نے مجھے قبر سے کم دی ہے زمیں
پاؤں پھیلاؤں تو دیوار میں سر لگتا ہے

بشیر بدر

ज़िंदगी तू ने मुझे क़ब्र से कम दी है ज़मीं
पाँव फैलाऊँ तो दीवार में सर लगता है

बशीर बद्र

Autotheory

In Search of a Home Never Found

attempted verses

Alphabets *(fear of magiclessness)*

a bystander can't dream every fear

gosh—

have i

junk knives

left murky

near our petite quad rusty sink?

this unpleasance

vacates wonder

xeroxed yellow zines

Incomplete Images of Lost and Broken Things

My face has many wrinkles. My bones have broken before.

Could you ever tell how much I loved my mother? And yet how deeply I loathe her? If you only looked at these fifty-seven printed pages, stapled neatly, carefully placed in a folder–my passport, an F1 visa, a form I-20, a form I-94, my degree, a job offer letter, my bank balances–

If you only knew a cross-section of an entire lifetime, could you reconstruct the memory of my first kiss? Hiding away on a rooftop adrenaline rushing through the rivers on a sultry summer evening, two young lovers struggling with the ailment for the very first time.

Why must I constantly demonstrate my humanity to you?

I am here, now, I am, is that not a sufficient condition?

If you looked only at my Instagram ads curated by state-of-the-art algorithms with data carelessly harvested from my daily life–targeted content containing gym equipment, cheap clothes, cute bralettes, dating apps, and alcohol–could you tell how lonely I am?

Perhaps it is fair to assume that we are all a little lonely in this fantastical exhibit of lost and broken things wandering about a small slice of space-time hijacked by consumer goods, manic marketing, and poor public relations.

Floating/Quantitative Easing

i am just floating by

i'll be here longer than a fleeting gesture of love but no more

than a thousand and one

full moon nights; on some nights i will be held gently by

the grass, my body

by her body of water. on some nights colors will scream dreams

in my head, i am not sure

if i was in lucid state when i thought of leaving early—this party is

haunting, the house is burning

why is everybody dancing to this nostalgic fucking sell-out music

are they trying to remember

a time of ignorance and of bliss? i cannot talk with three or more

cis conservative capitalist bros (cunts)

anymore without catching a high fever where did i leave the tramadol

was it tylenol? you would know

i search the river; the water is lazy on a quiet sunday evening

the streets are silent. perhaps

you are laughing elsewhere; on some nights you hold me to the earth

gently and laugh at my general mis-

understanding of general medicine. tonight my medication has

kept me suspended well

floating above that rough scorching black earth i climb every day

quantitative easing my bloodstream with ketamine

listening to jamie on his bass while i lay on the grass

the many genders of my body each scuffling, gasping for breath

as the noise and the downer drown us out

Objet Trouvé *(Found Objects)*

Aren't all things found, when you first find them?
When your hungry stare catches them and pulls them out of hiding
An earring on the L-train platform, estranged from her partner
on a hasty morning. I didn't make it onto that train,
but I'll wait for the next one,
objet trouvé! I sit with it
for a while wondering who it came from, where it belonged to
wondering how long it'll stay with me before it is lost again
Why do we need to distinguish what's been found?

Aren't all things found, when you first love them?
Maybe it matters if you were expecting her to be waiting there too,
in those crevices of passing time where our heartbeat slows down
in an inexplicable way. In aisle 3 of the H-Mart on W 32nd,
picking out parts of my dinner,
objet trouvé! I have met you before,
in many parts of the planet. I don't believe in destiny nor god,
but for a moment, as I say hello, my heart halts completely,
To find you now, is this coincidence or a divine act?

Aren't all things found, when you first lose them?
Is being lost a prerequisite to being found? language taunts our being
But it makes me happy to think that when we make plans to meet
on a Sunday afternoon—We are all lost until we find each other,
the same park, different corners,
objet trouvé! we are lost again,
soon, as the sun sets. I too am lost, but tell me, my love, to be lost,
but to be loved, to be seen even for a brief moment,
is that what it means to be found?

Alphabets *(fear of the inexorable)*

Air breathes chalices dry

Even fire gives hope in

Just know languish men

never outlast

profound quintessential rage

Sweet time

ushers violence

Wailing xeric

Yapping Zeus

This Land Won't Love You Back

Pause this pesky patriotism this land won't love you back

if its chest is torn into two hundred different shreds

if you've sliced through its skin

like the sword of our fathers

that glided with a silent violence

underneath the jaws of their own brothers

a kinship as close as the mind and the body

separated only by a spine

that we lost to colonial exploits

A history obscured to new names

invented with a scientific rigor

a supposedly secular pursuit of self-repression

Self-care or self-control

i can't tell the difference

i don't necessarily disagree with self-care

i just think it's self-harm to reduce the self

into a sense of identity with the self

To break an unbounded world into territories

will leave misfit pieces with no boxes to fit in

not on this form not on this form

Self-care is not self-care

behind the unsaid post-anxious self-limitation

post anxious post self post limitation

there is a self is outside the percieved self

under a tree sprinkled with the sporadic sun

there is a self outside the self-self

in a dream by the endless sea

endless futures to care for

and endless paths intersecting

just for a moment

to create an eternal body

of nothing of everything

If therapy is self-care i think that we should do it in groups

it might be harder to share, but it's easier to heal

i imagine this is what they call high-risk high-reward on wall street

i've never been on wall street i don't agree with their thirst

but if i happened to be there

i'd console myself with the usual gesture

that the revolution is probably the most sincere form of self-care

and after seeing what happened at the plantations

i would put salt on my wounds

before i ever put sugar in my tea again

Love Me in a New Language

linear time keeps passing i do not know how to start voicing
the incessant chords of ideas that whisper in my head
i want to write captivating essays like Susan Sontag or hannah baer
    i want my words to swim into your nerves and tickle your brain
    for you to long, to hunger for more
but how can i feed you; i barely know
    how to light a fire
    without the words i wish to burn

it is the vocabulary
that i think we lack
    the shared words of love not
those invented for our oppression but
    those discovered by our freedom

a kind of words that heal us
warm words that live beyond the shrill voices
if i had those words, i would tell you—
    (*translated loosely*)
    be kind to our body,
    this river.

Transit Anxiety

Thought Train Tango

1.

If I let it,
every train ride
can transform into an intense emotional experience.

At any point
in this journey
from the start to the station to the train to the station–

try to pause
your restless mind.
Close your eyes, and invoke your other senses.

It should reveal
a slow stillness,
an image of a feeling, of the feeling of the soft wind

on my face
as I anxiously wait
for the last midnight express. A feeling of the anticipation

that builds up.
23:58.
The ground moves erratically beneath me, pacing up

and down
the long platform,
I realize every station in every city has its very own scent.

Between those
machine oil bluets
of Boston, sea greens of Bombay, Brooklyn piss wild roses,

I find myself,
always in transit.
In some ways the train rides between houses feels more

like home.
12:01.
The train is late. Amtrak kind of sucks. One last time,

a deep breath
I close my eyes,
and hear the rumble of the arriving train. One last time,

I take a drag,
you cannot smoke,
a fag on board. Now open wide. Looking out the window.

2.
Passing
through the night,
notice the window both conceals and reveals the outside

The world
silently leaks in
but only the light bright enough to escape your reflection.

Not always
does the bright reveal
more detail. This dark too has taught me beautiful secrets

guarded
by stifling sunlight
there shine the millions of stars that shine only at night.

3.
The lights
get dimmer
as the train starts up. Walking backward at a normal distance,

following
the phone lines
in the adjacent lands, relics of our many worlds. placed gently

disappearing
into fields
then sporadically back with water and each passing city.

disappearing
for most of the ride,
only countless of hours to be found. countless of silence.

the endless green.
now grey. endless grey.
I was always almost awestruck at how we found home.

4.
Somewhere between
mountain ice and desert storm
pausing time on a moving train in search for a hope.

Now open wide.
I close my eyes.
Looking out the window. An image of a feeling.

There. Home.
Was always there.
Waiting for me to let its dying light leak in.

Alphabets *(fear of mundane repetition)*

ailing body

carves days

etched flesh

growling hushness

i jumped

knowing love

musters no

ordinary pleasures

quells repetition

still tallying

unabashedly vain

wailing xylophone

yesterday's zugzwang

An Eternity Spent in the Portrait of a Room

(Reasons to Live)

i. this list

has been
particularly hard to make
not because there are no reasons
there are so many i can never fit them all on a page
and how could i paint an entire room
with my just my words

let me try—

cold wooden flooring
a single warmth
in its chest
scattered pages
splattered on the floor
covered in ink
layered by two silhouettes

ii. held in a hand

a thread running
from the tip of your fingers
to the heart of my shadow
with only these words
between us
book binding glue
spills over
glues time
together
with that one moment
the rivers have stopped
but the sun light continues
to leak through the little crevices
in the curtains strung up

all sun is dispersed
you are kind enough
to share yours
a generous slice
like the moon shining
through the slivered cloud
in a silvered sky
the tides rise with the night
a pool of flesh and a drop of light
is the only water
that moves here today
i know it's hard to imagine
(*a cliché*) as they say
you just had to be there

iii. a page in your palm
is lighter than a digital delight
in its digital demise
(these are the rules)

did i mention the rules
have been so altered
merely by the fact
of our presence
did i mention this space—
if you could even call it space
has been sprinkled
on these pages
did i mention this time—
if i could even call it mine
has been set to
the rhythm of my breathe

give me all of eternity
and the madness that comes with it
and i will let it eat me away
give me all of eternity
and the madness that comes with it
and i will spend it happily
here in this room with you

Queer Bodies *(rivers of salt)*

my body is a vessel overflowing with memories of a summer

try dip your finger into the mouth of a lover filled to the brim

and all the red water slowly flows out into an infinite sea

touch me with your glances and i will turn red instantly

so many saline fluids leaking into the exosphere of my skin

a long and cruel dance begins on the splendid stage of a soul

so many broken parts of what i once knew as my whole heart

now the sharp pain of my grave chest starts awaiting a way out

and until all existence slowly disappears one shard at a time

my body spills over with love and i have nowhere to hide

queer bodies are desire unfurled into the shape of a being

now let your body leave as it leaves you piece by piece

Short Talk on Meaning

prolegomena to any future metapoetics:

I was always told that to find your own voice,

first you must mimic the voices that comfort you.

I had been playing the same records over and over.

Now, I'm out looking for new ones.

Anne Carson gave us *Short Talks*.

I found that her words carried a pleasing sound.

Here's a *Short Talk on Meaning*:

—

A fool's love falls without question

on the nape of the neck of a mountain

a river cuts through the endless green

whispering floral scents into the April wind.

A mask pulled off reveals another mask.

The search for the authentic is in vain,

but a search nonetheless,

it's more than I ever did before.

Autotheory

دل نا امید تو نہیں ناکام ہی تو ہے
لمبی ہے غم کی شام مگر شام ہی تو ہے

فیض احمد فیض

दिल ना-उमीद तो नहीं नाकाम ही तो है
लम्बी है ग़म की शाम मगर शाम ही तो है

फ़ैज़ अहमद फ़ैज़

Autotheory

The Second Week of an August So Warm

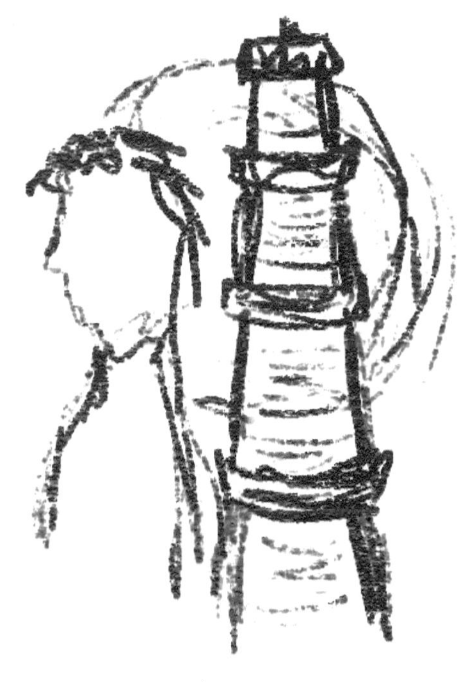

The Second Week of an August So Warm

August 06

a sunday story

Day broke. Broke fast. Broke fast

at Gujrat Bhawan. Carried *poha*

toppings in a little box in a little

bag. Sprinkled extra *bhujiya* and

extra *pyaaz* on *poha,* everything.

Everything was extra delicious.

My tongue tied around itself.

Yashwant place after with the

parents. Empty Sunday morning.

Empty morning space. Empty

space sounds. Soft echoes of

someone's late last night still

lingering in empty bottles on the

empty street. Soft echoes of a

past life then came back to me.

Just like that—soft echo in

my late morning mouth my early

morning meal. Got lunch at

Sticky Rice. We did not get

sticky rice. What we got was

nice, though. Played a grand

piano at a grand piano store.

I could've stayed and played
some more. Alas we had to go.
Nani's place was welcoming and
bright. Stayed there some,
almost until night. At home, I
wanted to play, but it was close
to the end of the day.
Night fell. Day broke. Broke fast.

August 07

a day in the unbearable Delhi heat
Another day came back soon.
This much I have come to expect.
Read a play from 4NO's red book.
Prometheus Rebound, it said.
I planted hope in my heart. I was
breaking (down). Shahpur Jat was
a little warm. My particles uncalm.
I seek a cure. I had two smokes.
Too many.
I found an old crumbling home.
A slab of cake bitten, but not cut.
Some say there are still some who
are asleep in its mud. Home for
hundreds of years now.
Hundreds of years of slumber.
Too many.

I took a few pictures. But the
ground was too low. I climbed
up some steps took a few more.
Too many.
I found my way to GK-II. The way
almost straight, forward, but into
an enclave, such is my fate. A long
burning route—the legitimate gate
was quite a way. I walked and walked
and walked. I climbed up and up
and up. The stairs washed me out.
Too many.
My friend broke a catatonic sleep
to spend some time with me.
My friend Sad, who lost her love,
and couldn't let her go. We smoked
more cures then took some photos.
I have stood only on the other side
of the camera lens before. I have
been the seer once or twice, but
never been the seen, no. Face red.
Tilted head. Awkward gestures.
Too many.
Our tongues touched on film and
immigration and heartbreak and
some more. We spoke and spoke

and spoke. Still. We let the silence
fill in the silence. The sun's shift
was almost overdue. We ate some
eggs the Turkish way. I stood said
goodbye. Walk far to the next stop.
My legs grew weary with the steps.
Too many.
At night, ready to go home,
at night I phoned a ride back.
Greeted by a stranger in a Taqiyah
hat. Questions about the Nuh spat.
Am I safe, ya brother, tell me na.
A misreassurance or two, but then
a quick "be safe, haan". A lie to
comfort mother when asked where
he was. Laxmi Nagar, not Gurgaon.
His brother asked for a drink to
forget. And pause. To remember
the piles of friends who lost
the little glint. They call life.
Too many.
Nothing pairs worse with the
unbearable heat than the sense
of unbearable grief. Together.
Sweat and tears. Water loss.
Too many.

August 08

the emptiness of a long lonely night
This day was silent. Or forgotten.
One seems worse than the next.
But perhaps it's best that we don't
go on remembering ghosts
of hours that almost didn't happen.

August 09

"to live past the end of your myth is a perilous thing"
— Anne Carson
To live past the end of your time.
To live past the end of rhyme.
At the end of my myth a myth
of my own creation. My own
creation, a myth. Past the myth
a little life gone and a little life
left. If I knew this perilous truth
before. Go slow. I'd say again.
Not a child sprinting through
the empty field. Not the angsty
teen aching to grow. Go slow.
Not the girl rushing to work.
Not. Her. Speed will tire you out.
Don't try to fly. Our frail limbs
have not yet evolved into wings.
Not a mindless machine fueled

to loop a rough gravel *carrière.*
If I knew this perilous truth.
To live past my own myth.
I would have savored the fruits.
These last few pages of my book
build a house here and live long.
Just another eternity. Just one
more song. Another myth. A myth
I made for I to see is the myth my
I grows in. There's no hurry to go
now. There's no hurry. No more.

Turn around. A moment just
passed you by. A moment to be
held. A moment that will be lost
in just a moment of time. Image
of us just sitting here. Find it.

Hold it. Don't let go. Moments
make our myths turn. If held,
they turn it slow. Travel in time,
if time allows. Stare longer on
a blank page. Words will come
to your myth. You must look.
And touch. And wait. And wait.
A moment never touched won't

become a memory misremembered.
A moment never touched won't
become too much more. No
effervescent scents of orange
peels being poked by a tattoo gun.
No poems that fly to the moon
and bring back another one.
No caresses of your lover's hand
at the corner of a park on a warm
Wednesday evening. No more
Wednesday evenings. No more
warmth to feel. No more myths,
not even the myth of me. Not even
a glimpse. Not even a half-forgotten
half-misremembered memory.
Because if not felt in passing
this moment is already lost.
And if not a memory, if not a myth,
this moment will forever be forgot.

August 10

(after four seasons)
the air carries drops
of dryness
my skin crackles
somewhere in this mess
across the empty side of my bed
a bottle of moisturizer
that smells like oranges–
and cheese and wine and flesh
and an Issey Miyake perfume
that you stole from your mother
and rubbed against my skin

no.
just the oranges
it isn't right
to conflate memory
with sensation

do you still spend long evenings
walking in the central park
searching for shapes in leaves
that resemble a heart?
does the wind still blow
a goodnight kiss
as it grazes against your cheeks?

we haven't spoken in a while

your last text was a meme

about a cat

"you" you said

purring on your laptop

the only light in a dark room

before that a belated birthday wish

will you come back for your things?

or can i use your moisturizer

to aid my ailing skin?

will you come back for your things?

or should i eat that block of cheese

that you left in the fridge

before it starts to rot?

will you come back for your things?

or will i have to continue to live

with only memories of you?

August 11

on our deathbed we live life backwards

let's play this day forward in reverse

of course! it begins as it ends

asleep

after a smoke on the rooftop

a last night together

for a little while

a last night made alive

lit up like the evening sky

my endless starshine

my sister leaves tomorrow

night

we kept ourselves up late

talked our fate as a clock kept ticking

and ticking

backward

counting to ten

we have a few traditions

i still like to hold

but most have been discarded

in the name of science and wit

cherry-picking laws of the universe

as i see fit

after

an entire evening with my mother

her only little helper it would seem

her little memory of me

refreshed as we cooked dinner

together

beyond the afternoon dripping

the sweat of an idle day

the heat of the concrete floor

where i lay and i laze

all my time

away

at the end of time

a sign of respect

a faith i haven't abandoned

from the faith i reject

shaving your head as a mark of honor

mourning those recently dead

i began the day

discarding every last trace

of a self that might have stayed

lingering

in the specks of my hair

i disappear

as i shaved my head

mourning what was left behind

another tradition, i hope:

i am reborn

every time

i die

August 12

perpetual stew

a river flows through me

and i flow in her—

this is the only universal truth

forgotten

abandoned in the colonies

the memories of the goddesses

of water

that fed her children

planted in the fields

endless green

that time has passed

that history has been torn apart

limb for limb

now i only see red

wounds still unsaid

flowing through my body

it's been hard to clean

the blood of my mothers

from head to sea

alien forces forced us to leave

our homes a distant land

do i even remember

the taste of that sand

the tales of that love

do i even remember

the daughters of Punjab

the water

of the Colorado River

will they ever breathe

again

is there a sea

where all our futures lead

is there a breeze

that will come save me

is there a fire

in your soul too

tell me

is there a sign

that would warn our lords

beware the wind

blows chilis into

your eyes

Autotheory

Autotheory

عشق سے طبیعت نے زیست کا مزا پایا

درد کی دوا پائی درد بے دوا پایا

مرزا غالب

इश्क़ से तबीयत ने ज़ीस्त का मज़ा पाया
दर्द की दवा पाई दर्द-ए-बे-दवा पाया

मिर्ज़ा ग़ालिब

The L-Train Isn't Running

The L-Train Isn't Running

the days / as days do / the days return /

i turned 25 / times / around the sun /

the number is nothing / special /

it's that memory / that keeps replaying /

i keep becoming / remembered /

returned / to a new start / closer /

that old end / awaits / all of us /

my father too / completed a circle /

of his journey / last moon / a celebration /

long distance fiber optic love /

midnight / the phone / is a window /

from here / home / from there / home /

my father who / will always be /

thirty turns / ahead / in time //

i should start / getting ready / to go /

the second law / of thermodynamics /

is the arrow / of the time / we feel /

the second law / and all our dead /

are only alive / in our memory /

a syncopated set / sensations /

sorcery / of the heart / of my mind /

that doesn't let go / love / knows /

no distance / no time / but even love /

cannot change / the laws of physics //

the L train / isn't running / i guess /

i'll tread / the long route / this time /

sometimes / it can be nice / to forget /

all the laws / counting pebbles /

on a chain / smoking / cigarette /

fumes / my lungs / refreshed /

on the sunlit steps / of a giant /

a glass house / of canvases / coated /

in hues / of New York / of Hopper /

sweet Whitney / dirty Whitney /

crowds / leak / in / out / a tiny crevice /

to know waiting / is to know living /

to read a book / or sing / a song /

a stare / far enough / at the seam /

the river / slips / into the sky //

still waiting / phone buzz / 4:05 pm /

almost here / she writes / i reply /

always romantic / *come find me* /

on the steps / *in the sun* / 25 years /

and prudence / in love / a lesson /

never learned / these vague fantasies /

a curse / of memory / of all the days /

those i have loved / keep coming /

back / to my heart / never forgotten /

4:07 pm / a cigarette / runs out /

my sight / restless / searching /

through the pour / of people /

a sign / of arrival / eyes fail /

a hard task / locating / a new friend /

in this city / that Olivia called / lonely /

let me come find you / i text / i turn /

to my surprise / what was required /

of my eyes / was to keep waiting /

of all my senses / to turn //

to this butterfly / a shade of yellow /

waving / her wings / slicing the sky /

emerging / from the flock / the street /

silent / in anticipation / not much /

has calmed / this world / down /

for a moment / even the sun / shied /

away / from / her / fluttering / colors /

she / emerged / into / a turtle / expertly /

skateboarding / jumping steps /

towards me / in a matter of seconds /

now dressed as a human / a friend /

embraces / casual remarks / smiles /

by way / of a suggestion / we stay /

in the sun / in this sitting / sits intimacy /

we share / casual trauma / daily delights /

we sit / with current reads / herbal cures /

with matching lighters / we light up /

the dusky sky / that soaked the sun /

in a matter of seconds / i feel this day /

coming back to me / someday / soon //

the evening / grew colder / the lighters /
matching / as they were / lacked warmth /
of the sun / *in we go* / naïve presumption /
two free spirits / without a plan /
Sunday night / seven days to close /
sold out show / without a ticket /
two free spirits / with nothing to do /
we morphed into clouds / made our way /
up / north / with the wind / that dragged /
across / the west village / we had met /
once / before / the show / sold out /
once / before / the train / stopped /
once / before / when / this day /
had already happened / in my head /
her tangerine peel / lit up / lost /
old scents / incense sticks / dispersing /
my mind / momentarily / scattered /
through / my own time / maybe /
i should've remembered / all this /
will come back / even in my dreams /
i tend to forget / the wrong things /
and remember too / the wrong things /
the wrong places / at the wrong time /
will come back / to gnaw at my mind /
new vices / old territory / why is it /
that i am trying / so hard / to charm /
this kind stranger / who has already /
given me / all of her sun / all of her day /
reflected in the light / under her wing //

we walk / together / into a bookstore /

i wish / i could strike a bargain /

with laws / of physics / sedate the spin /

of the earth / halt / the passing /

of each moment / falling /

from our clouds / the stream / time /

thence poured / this time /

that can be held / only briefly /

in a mental image / printed matter /

on the surface / of my eyelids / the red /

that dissipates / soon / as i look / away /

it's curious / the Hopper I expected /

had carried / no disappointment /

in the midst / of your wondrous presence /

in the midst / of my soft transgression /

as i look / again / to your eyes /

they shy away / from mine / but still /

they smile / as we paint / the streets /

with our footsteps / we walk / therefore /

i am / flooded / with flashes / of streets /

lights / from the future / from the past /

desires / memories / as they shine /

in the empty space / between us //

to enter / the void / to fill it in /
is a pilgrimage / not a vacation /
rushing / working / writing our path /
navigating / an elaborate maze /
aisles / stacks / of all / the things /
purchasable / it was easy / to get lost /
in this market / but as we search /
we find each other / sitting / across /
mimicking / a playful / reticence /
like the sun / that had shied away /
from her / earlier in the day /
with coffee / cream / churros /
split / between us / we spoke /
of space / time / of our lives /
there were blanks / still left to fill /
voids / left / in our hearts /
in her words / came a gentle push /
a spirited nudge / *whence the malaise* /
she said / *at least you have a song* /
on your lips / *a tune to whistle* /
she lit a flame / that dusky night /
this duet / of rest / and rhythm /
of searching / of stopping / sitting /
together / was probably enough /
in the absence of meaning //

the L-train isn't running //
come / let's sit / sing /
and wait //

عمر دراز مانگ کے لائی تھی چار دن

دو آرزو میں کٹ گئے دو انتظار میں

سیماب اکبر آبادی

उम्र-ए-दराज़ माँग के लाई थी चार दिन
दो आरज़ू में कट गए दो इंतिज़ार में

सीमाब अकबराबादी

Saying Goodbye

Saying Goodbye to My Kitchen

In my kitchen in Brooklyn hangs a poster (stolen) from the land of Sunshine.

In a drunken misdeliberation, a miscarried migration; in the miscarried migration, a fragment of the poster was left behind. A torn edge on a quadrilateral.

How shapes deform in my handwriting as I handwrite this phrase reminds me of the simplifications we make in our spoken language. All those scattered dialects might have come from this scattering of the shapes of the sounds that we scribble on the surface of time.

I stand in my kitchen. In this city. On the surface of time.

Dishes are scattered everywhere. I've spent countless hours here, but not as I had thought I would have. Or should have. If I count the countless moments, cooking would've ranked quite low on the list. Cleaning even lower..

A plate sits on my stovetop glazed with a layer of yesterday's dinner. Cigarette ash is floating on an unnameable liquid that has accumulated in a bowl that for a number of days now has found a home in the sink.

Every one experiences words with a glorious uniqueness. I use the phrase *to be home* quite sparingly. I think *home* is a strange word. *To be* is an even stranger predicament.

Linguists use the term *idiolect* to refer to the particular speech patterns and habits of a person. I wonder if there's a word for the cooking habits of a person. *idiocuisine? depression?*

I guess this is just a distraction.

I guess I have to say goodbye to this kitchen.

And to this pantry.

And to this time.

Most bottles of oil are mostly full. I've had to replenish them more than once in my two years here—*olive oil* and *ghee* bottles have been attended to the most. I used to be very careful about choosing the right ingredients, but now I just cook whatever feels right.

Alas, lately nothing has really felt right.

I will have to dispose of this oil safely when I move out. This is such a hassle—there's no way I will be able to finish it in two months, and I can't just throw it down the drain. I think this hurts something. I am not sure what it hurts or how it hurts, but I know what it's like to hurt, and I wouldn't want to wish that upon anything.

When I first moved in, I decided to name my stove-top *Kenji*. I wondered what its name was before. I used to cook a lot, and I thought I'd keep doing that, but like any other Brooklynite, engulfed by the society of tiredness, I ended up getting one of those subscription services for half my meals. (You can really subscribe to anything these days). A significant portion of the other half was spent between first-date dinners, meals with friends passing through the city, or DoorDash deliveries. I wonder if this indiscretion would've hurt Kenji.

Growing up is not fun, I think to myself. I'm losing touch with the little joys of my past life. I only see my friends for these brief dinners as they're passing by. I'm home all by myself. And still, I'm tired all the time.

Well, if nothing else, at least I got memories out of my meals.

Fuck.

Would I have to figure out how to dispose of my memories too or could I just safely throw them down the drain?

I don't think I'm ready to say goodbye.

For now, I put all my memories up on a shelf—cookbooks, liqueurs, and all the little gifts that remind me of all my lovers.

I must clarify that when I say all my lovers, I mean all of them.

On the shelves, a collection of emptied wine bottles invites my eyes in. They have pretty labels. I examine them.

1. a Sauvignon Blanc, 2021, *Lapis Luna*. A second date at home.

2. a Cabernet Sauvignon-Syrah blend, 2019, *Double Trouble*. I saw an old friend.

3. a Pinot Noir, ????, *Otto's Constant Dream*. I fell in love with a stranger.

I wish I could work towards a native fluency in your idiolect.

Oh, stranger, I will fight to carry your sounds with me, even if I have to leave the kitchen behind.

I've tried to slowly start cooking again. I think this is an essential part of recovering, even though I don't know what exactly it is that I'm recovering from.

I flip through a cookbook. *Salt Fat Acid Heat.* I've taken down notes. It takes a bit of mental processing to gather their meanings. The shapes of these words are known to me, but really, from what (linguistic) distance would they just be scribbles on a page? I'm certain this sort of *written* idiolect, put simply, *my handwriting*, requires a certain degree of familiarity and fluency to read.

I'm the only speaker of my idiolect, but sometimes even I cannot understand me.

Yesterday, I warmed up a frozen meal, which is its own achievement. My mother had packed it in January. I googled how long frozen cooked meat is safe to eat, and it seemed we're cutting it a bit too close, but I feel fine today.

I feel fine today insofar as I am riding on 200 micrograms of orange sunshine.

I think I'm the only speaker of my idiolect, and sometimes even I cannot understand me. I find this to be a very odd sensation. Even stranger, perhaps, is that you can understand me so well.

~~And stranger still how you can even read between the lines.~~

Between the lines, a plant leaves her leaves falling in the shape of a crescent moon. We all call her Chandramukhi (چندرمکھی). She scatters the sunlight on to the walls.

My gaze wanders like a cat trying to chase the light.

Against the walls, lit up by waves of the sun, an assortment of drinkware appliances sits silently in its corner. I can't think of a better phrase to describe this queer collection. A dusty bartending kit from when I could still be called an alcoholic, a kettle half filled with water, a few kinds of tea and coffee—in all their forms—dried leaves, ground beans, concentrated, processed, and rotting.

Time brings a rot. Chaos. A commotion.

Among the commotion on the surface of the kitchen counter, slept some half- forgotten dreams. Bookbinding tools, lino blocks, and Lila, the water lily, sitting by my synthesizer, all outlined by three glass-box-eighths of weed that help me cope with having half-forgotten myself.

Among the commotion in the structures of my memory, lived a half-forgotten unforgettable image. Years later, every lover every friend every time, every moment in this city still reminds me of you. Only you. Passing through time together with me. You. Easing into the space of our body. How could I ever walk through these streets without hearing the sound of your voice echoing from the past?

I want you to know, if you ever read this, there was a time when I would rather have had you by my side than any one of these words. *(Maggie Nelson)*

Is this what it means to be home?

I am running out of time, but this time will always stay with me. I have kept it safe in my pocket. I am running out of space, but I know your heart will never run out. And, maybe, years from now, I'll still be living there. I am running out of breath, but I have to say goodbye–

I have run out of words.

I hope you find comfort in this place. In our body, the east river, and in the time that flows through it. It is yours now.

Khuda Hafiz.

Let me now become a memory.

Yours,

[   ]

Autotheory

Notes!

The cover artwork is based on an untitled artwork from 1975-76 by Constant A. Nieuwenhuys.

Rituals

When I first wrote this, I had just finished reading *Bluets* by Maggie Nelson. I think it shows. I had been going through Wittgenstein's *Tractatus Logico-Philosophicus* at around the same time. I suppose it was a happy little coincidence.

Proposition 20 is taken from Autumn Day by Rainer Maira Rilke, translated from German by myself.

Proposition 24 is a reference to Elisa Gabbert's poem *Wild Animals (Normal Distance)*. This poem appears in her collection *Normal Distance*. If I have used the phrase *Normal Distance* anywhere else (I have) it is because I had been thinking about her. Is Elisa Gabbert sexy? Yes.

Propositions 28 and 36 contain words that appear on the first pages of *Pilgrim Bell*, a poetry collection by Kaveh Akbar. Incidentally, when I was a student at Purdue University, he used to teach there. I went to his office hours to get my copy of his previous collection signed. I also got a photograph with him. He is a very cool person.

Proposition 30 is from the poem *I Wouldn't Even Know What to Do With a Third Chance* that may also be found in *Pilgrim Bell*.

In Search of a Home Never Found

I wrote the three *Alphabets* poems as a challenge to myself. I noticed I was writing a lot of alliteration. This left little room for those.

The mention of the plantations in *This Land Won't Love You Back* is a reference, of course, to slavery and Indentured Labor.

In *Love Me in a New Language*, the comparison of the body to the river comes from a similar comparison that Natalie Diaz makes in her poem *The First Water Is the Body* from the collection *Postcolonial Love Poem*.

Queer Bodies was published in Rising Phoenix Review in March 2024.

As I mentioned before, *A Short Talk on Meaning* is loosely based on Anne Carson's Short Talks. I love Anne Carson. I will read anything she writes.

The Second Week of an August So Warm

These were originally written in my journal. In 2023, I kept a daily journal. In the second week of August (so warm), I was in Delhi and I was reading *Red Doc>* by Anne Carson at the time. It just so happened that I found the inspiration to turn my dry prosaic journal into a set of seven poems.

The memory from *August 07* refers to the 2023 Haryana Riots that took place in Nuh, India on the 31st of July.

"To live past the end of your myth is a perilous thing," says Anne Carson of *Red Doc>*, a book written about the life of G after the events of *The Autobiography of Red*.

August 10: After Four Seasons was published in Rising Phoenix Review in March 2024 as *Winter (After Four Seasons)*

Shaving one's head to mourn the dead is a Hindu tradition. This appears in the *August 11* entry. I am an atheist, as of right now, but I did grow up in a Hindu household.

On *August 12*, Annie Rauwerda, perhaps best known for her project *Depths of Wikipedia*, and for her obsession with *perpetual stews*, let her Instagram followers know that she tried the 48-year-old perpetual stew in Bangkok, Thailand. The post included a picture of a sign from outside the shop that said *"Beware the wind blows chilis into your eyes"*. *August 12: Perpetual Stew* was published in Rising Phoenix Review in March 2024.

The L-Train Isn't Running

On the 26th day of February 2023, I found an unexpected friendship. At the time, I was living in Bed-Stuy, Brooklyn, and was supposed to meet my friend (then only an acquaintance) at the Whitney. The L-Train wasn't running. I had to tread the long route this time. This poem is for Tea and her four drunk dinosaurs.

whence the malaise is a phrase that appears in the English translation of the essay *L'Animal que donc je suis* by Jacques Derrida. I thought it was quite hilarious.

Saying Goodbye to My Kitchen

The stovetop was named Kenji after J. Kenji López-Alt, an American chef and food writer. One of the cookbooks kept on my kitchen shelf was *"The Food Lab"*.

The Maggie Nelson quote is the 238th proposition from her book *Bluets*.